Hope and Miracles

Stories that Inspire

Forward by Paula Beiger

All proceeds from the sale of this book will be donated to Let There Be Health, A NJ Non-Profit Corporation PO Box 3462, Mercerville, NJ 08619

DISCLAIMER: The techniques and suggestions expressed here are intended to be used for educational and entertainment purposes only. We do not intend to render medical advice, nor to diagnose, prescribe or treat any disease, condition or illness. It is recommended before beginning any nutrition or exercise program you receive clearance from your physician.

First Edition Printed November 2019

ISBN 9781693405549

Cover Design by
Thomas Kelly

Edited by
Dennis C. Duffy

Table of Contents

Acknowledgments

Like the 1967 Letterman song, *No Man Is An Island*, this life changing project took many people to complete.

I'd like to thank all of the authors who were brave enough to share their stories: Dave Hart, Pearl Kennedy, Gina Di Iorio, Mary Theresa Donegan-Weil, Mickey Gordon, Gilda Rorro, William Sheehan, Kristin Perilli, Christine O'Shea and Maria Remboski. Thank you to Denita Stevens for providing the opening poem and Nora Riley for the closing meditation.

I am indebted to Dennis Duffy, who edited *Hope and Miracles*. As an editor, you not only check facts, spelling, grammar and punctuation, but you polish and refine a story, sometimes turning a block of words into a free-flowing story. Thanks to Dennis' touch, these stories are as close to perfection as possible.

A big thank you goes out to my friend, Dave Hart, who I called for advice when I became overwhelmed. After speaking with Dave, my confidence grew. Thanks for always making me feel like I can accomplish anything. To make people feel unstoppable is a gift.

Thank you and I love you to my husband Jack Beiger, who sees me at my best and at my worst and loves me anyway. My courage, my strength, my never give up attitude comes from having the unwavering, unconditional love and support of this amazing man. Oh, and he formatted the entire book.

I'm grateful to the printing sponsors: Dr. Mark James Bartiss of Institute of Complementary and Alternative Medicine (ICAM) in Whiting, NJ; Lisa and Greg Blair of Robbinsville, NJ; and Keller Williams Premier of Robbinsville, NJ. Because of their generosity, 100% of the sales of *Hope and Miracles* will be used to ease the financial burden individuals diagnosed with cancer experience.

The startling facts are, 42% of cancer patients lose their life savings and 62% of cancer patients report being in debt due to their treatments.

The *Let There Be Health* non-profit is grateful that we're able to help.

Foreword

Most everyone has a calling of some sort, some large, some small. There are those who seek it out, while others have one that finds them. In my case, not only did mine find me, but it put me in the path of an expanded calling, one which I would never have imagined for myself but have answered with a vigor I never knew I possessed. Allow me to briefly relate my story, which brought me to this most unexpected and most rewarding calling in my life.

It's a sunny day and I can see my husband, Jack, in the distance, walking toward the car from the Indian market located in the BAPS Shri Swaminarayan Mandir. The Mandir is in the neighboring town of Robbinsville, not far from my home. The parking lot is a football field away from the massive, 60,000 cubic feet of mesmerizing, imported marble. The Temple is an amazing representation of Indian culture. Its architectural design is a chiseled work of art.

The market is open to the public and imports products from India. We routinely buy our Neem toothpaste there. Since my cancer diagnosis, we try to eliminate as many chemicals as possible. Neem toothpaste is fluoride free.

As Jack reaches the car, I feel my phone vibrating against my leg. The call is from Virginia Beach.

"Hello."

"Hi. Paula?"

"Yes, it's Paula."

"Hi, it's Dawn Higgins Andrews, we're members of Chris Wark's SQ1 Support Group on Facebook. Do you remember me?"

"Oh, yes. Hi, Dawn. Yeah, we've had a couple text conversations."

"Yes, I love your story and I love that you've published a book that details how you healed from stage III Colon cancer naturally."

Jack can hear the conversation, since I have Dawn on speakerphone. At this point, I'm smiling at Jack and pointing to the phone, with an excited expression on my face.

I tell Dawn, "I love your story, too."

Dawn had breast cancer. She healed with conventional treatments. Within a year, the cancer returned. Now, she is healing naturally.

Dawn continues, "In the fall, I'm having an event at the Museum of Contemporary Art in Virginia Beach called *Rise Up for Healing.* I'm hoping you can come and be our 'Keynote Speaker'."

Now, Jack and I are looking at each other with eyes widened. My lips are silently mouthing, 'Keynote Speaker!' I try to contain the excitement in my voice.

"Dawn, I'd love to! I know by your posts in SQ1 that we're on the same page about natural healing."

For the fifteen minutes it takes Jack and me to reach home, Dawn and I talk like we're old high school girlfriends. By the end of our conversation, I'm excited and terrified at the same time because Dawn is giving me the opportunity to speak in front of a large audience.

Fast-forward to the *Rise Up for Healing* event. It is amazing. Dawn did a phenomenal job of bringing together like-minded people, who want to teach that we have choices when it comes to healthcare. There's an expo type reception with community partners who empower you with their knowledge about natural healing.

After the reception, the program begins. First, Dawn's awesome teenage daughter, Morgan, does an interpretive dance as a tribute to her mother's healing. It's amazing!

Then it's my turn to speak, to be followed by Dr. David MacDonald, Doctor of Osteopathy, Board Certified Family Physician and President of the Liberty Health Group. I'm speaking in good company.

Dawn introduces me. My heart begins beating out of my chest. I'm in an auditorium with hundreds of people and it's the biggest stage I've ever been on. I'm very new at public speaking so I have my speech, in writing, in a binder. Fortunately, there's a music stand for me to place my binder upon.

Oh my God! The binder doesn't fit well on the stand.

Oh no! Dawn's notes fell off the stand.

I bend over to pick up the notes. I recall the last thing Jack said to me after I got dressed, "You look fabulous! You're going to be great!" But then added, "Whatever you do, don't bend over. People will see your underwear."

I practiced this speech so many times. I know this story. I lived this story. I don't need this written copy.

Then, I freeze!

"Did someone see my underwear?"

I start to read my speech, word for word. *Will my mind calm down? OK, everybody's laughing at the right spots. I can do this.* How can one's mind be doing so many different things all at once? *I can't wait for this 20-minute speech to be over. Finally.......... I did it! I finished... And they clapped.*

11

Of course, Jack said it was wonderful. And so did my friend, Denita.

Oh, yeah. I forgot to tell you my new Texas girlfriend came on this adventure with us. I met Denita in the Hamilton Library Writers' Group. We became quick friends and I'm excited to tell you Denita Stevens introduces *Hope and Miracles* with an original poem made especially for the book.

It's Dr. MacDonald's turn to speak. He's a great orator who doesn't use any notes. He makes me feel I've done a good job on stage, referencing things I had said, agreeing with all of it and acknowledging me in the audience with a polite gesture.

I guess if the words are right, it doesn't matter about the performance. Everyone seems interested in hearing how I healed from stage III Colon cancer in 20 months, naturally.

Having the speeches and the Q & A with Dr. MacDonald completed, Jack has a juice demonstration out in the lobby, which everyone enjoys and where a majority of the audience buys my book, *Guided Cure*.

All in all, it's a success.

Afterward, having driven 300 miles for the event, we turned the trip into a mini vacation. We enjoyed Virginia Beach, taking pictures at the huge statue of King Neptune, touring old fisherman houses and going to the Edgar Cayce Museum.

Ironically, Edgar Cayce is known as the Father of Holistic Medicine, as well as the 'Miracle Man' of Virginia Beach. His family claims he was best known for the nearly 14,000 mystical readings he delivered during his lifetime, all while in an apparent sleep induced or hypnotic state. They called him the 'Sleeping Prophet'.

One of Edgar Cayce's quotes was: "You get to Heaven on the arms of the people you have helped."

Driving home from Virginia Beach, we discover the 'Million Dollar Mile'. We're riding along, happily, and all of a sudden, we get pulled over by a State Trooper in Virginia. Jack pulls to the side of the road and the officer walks up to the window and asks Jack, "Do you know what you were doing, sir?"

"No, officer. Is one of my lights out?" Jack responds.

"No, Sir. You were going 14 miles over the speed limit."

"Oh, I didn't realize that. I was just trying to pass the tractor trailer." Jack tells the officer.

"No problem, sir," the officer assured us, tapping Jack's Veteran's bumper sticker. "I'm going to take good care of you."

Casually returning from his car, the officer hands Jack a $175 ticket, then has the audacity to say, "Enjoy the rest of your trip home and obey the speed limits." For the next 10 miles, we try to figure out how it was he took care of Jack. Is going over the speed limit by 14 miles an hour while passing the tractor trailer punishable by jail time in Virginia? With no consensus reached, we arrive home safely without another incident.

Jack will pay the ticket. He can let it go.

Not me… it keeps popping up in my head over and over again. That $175 ticket is a thorn in my side.

That first night home, I awake in the middle of the night. Boom! My head's off the pillow and I'm instantly in the sitting-up position. The words *Let There Be Health* keep ringing in my head. I can't get back to sleep, my mind is racing… 14 miles over the speed limit. Ha!

I think to myself, *"Why are we traveling so far to spread the good news of the choices we have when it comes to health? We could spread the news right here in New Jersey."*

I loved the event in Virginia Beach, but I realize I could put on an event like that right here in my home state. I could get community partners. I could get doctors to speak about complementary and alternative modalities. And that's exactly what I did.

That very morning, I called four professional women whom I knew felt the same way as I did about health. On November 3, 2018, we held the inaugural *Let There Be Health* conference, with 28 community partners and two doctors to speak, Dr. Mark Bartiss and Dr. Eric Jaszewski. There were three speakers who gave testimony on how they healed naturally from PTSD, heart disease and head injuries, plus yours truly to speak about healing from stage III Colon cancer.

There were over 200 attendees at the conference, confirming our beliefs that people are open to learning more about complementary and alternative modalities.

Here is a quick summary:

December 2011 - Diagnosed with stage III Colon cancer.

October 21, 2013 - Deemed cancer free, naturally.

February 2017 - Published the book *Guided Cure,* detailing how I healed in 20 months, naturally.

November 2018 - Created a conference called *Let There Be Health* to share the choices one has when it comes to healing.

June 17, 2019 - Founded *Let There Be Health* 501(c) (3) non-profit corporation to aid people who experience financial burden when diagnosed with cancer.

They say God doesn't pick the most qualified to do his work. That is certainly true in this case, for nothing I've done in the past eight years was ever on my bucket list. However, I do, now, consciously put things on my bucket list.

I have learned to surround myself with brilliant people. Please read the acknowledgments.

In closing, let's go back to a quote from the Father of Holistic Medicine, Edgar Cayce, "You get to Heaven on the arms of the people you have helped."

100% of the proceeds of the book *Hope and Miracles* will be going to, *Let There Be Health*, a NJ 501(c) (3) non-profit, to aid individuals who experience financial burden when a family receives a cancer diagnosis.

Stories heal. I hope those in this book inspire you as they have inspired me. We all have a story to tell. Tell your story. It could be exactly what someone else needs to hear to give them hope and help them heal.

Miracles happen – Paula Beiger

Shout Out

As a result of a cancer diagnosis, sister-thriver Natasha 'Tash' Blum became my virtual Facebook friend.

It amazes me how the Internet brings communities together. Tash made the logo for Dawn's *Rise Up for Healing* event. We were introduced at that event, but not in person. Tash could not attend.

We ultimately established an on-line relationship when Tash joined with Lisa Karen to form *The Boss Beauties Online Academy*.

This academy helps women 'do it differently' when promoting their businesses on-line. *BossBeauties* is 'classy, sassy and a little bad-assy'. Tash and Lisa Karen taught me everything I know about promoting events, including the new, non-profit *Let There Be Health* on-line.

Thank you, Beauties!!

I hope y'all check them out. #BossBeauties

Tell them Paula sent you.

Dedication

I'm dedicating this book to **Kristin Muir**, a fellow cancer warrior, who passed on November 4, 2019. I was inspired by her when she courageously shared her story on Facebook. Her story was my story: the struggles, the fears, the setbacks, the tears and the financial burdens. But for some reason, I couldn't talk about it publicly. It was easier for me to stay in denial about the financial difficulties we experienced.

While God was blessing me with healing, we were lucky we didn't lose our house in the process. Kristin's vulnerability in telling her story unabashedly inspired me, giving me the motivation to make *Let There Be Health,* 501(c) (3) non-profit corporation a reality. Thank you, Kristin. You're one of my heroes.

About the Cover

In late August I contacted local artist, Thomas Kelly, with an idea about the cover of this book. Giving him the name *Hope and Miracles*.

I told him, "When people look at the cover, I want them to feel joy, innocence, happiness and bliss."

I showed him two pictures I felt invoked these feelings and asked him to put his creative spin on it. He asked me about the background of one of the pictures and I told him, "You can't tell in the picture, but the subject is going down a big slide."

Even though Tom was busy with end-of-summer vacations with his wife, Linda and three children, a son heading off to his first year of college and beautiful twin girls going off to high school, he quickly responded, "Sounds interesting. Let me see what I can come up with."

Two and a half weeks later, I received a text with a pencil sketch that brought me to tears. I loved it! There was an explanation from Tom that read, "Paula, I love the sliding board idea. I feel the joys and memories from school playgrounds are deeply embedded within all of us. The slide was a wondrous and very brave thing for little ones.

I wish to portray a little girl on the slide, fearless as she goes down, he continued. At the bottom, a huge pile of pillows in all shapes and colors, as if we all would do anything we could to protect this child. A tree in the background symbolizes a long life and strength. The child would be joyful and unafraid......Do you have a main color in mind? His text asked.

Thanks. Please let me know your thoughts."

I told Tom, I was thrilled with it and use his own discretion with the color selection. A short while later, I was presented with this colorful masterpiece.

Not only am I excited about the ten inspirational stories, the opening poem and the ending meditation in this book, I'm excited the cover is a 'true' work of art!

Thank you, Tom for accepting the challenge.

Cover Design by Thomas Kelly

Thomas Kelly is an award-winning New Jersey based painter. Widely collected, his work has a signature style which has its roots in expressionism. His colorful, narrative, acrylic paintings on canvas often create a dialogue with the viewer. His deceptively simplistic paintings are both critically acclaimed and very popular with everyday viewers. More than 250 original paintings of Tom's have been collected, 80% of the paintings Tom has created.

Tom works from small sketches and, as he says, "My tiny original sketch can usually be overlaid right onto the finished painting. That is how close I stick to the original idea. That is what I wish to portray, that raw sketch is what first fascinated me."

Tom states, "I am not and do not wish to be the artist with the best technical skill, recreating realism that wows the masses. I wish to be the one who connects well with the way people feel. I wish to have the viewer say about themselves, when they see my art, *"This is about me, this is about my life."* This is how I wish to connect. The universal feelings we all have is what I am trying to portray. "

Kelly is represented regionally by 4 galleries. Please see www.thomaskellyart.com for more information.

About the Editor

Dennis C. Duffy is an architect and graduate of Drexel University in Philadelphia who has turned his interests to writing and editing. His edits include Paula Beiger's *Guided Cure*, as well as various articles and periodicals. His short story, *Nightly Visits*, was published a few years ago and he has compiled a number of original short stories, seeking to publish them as a collection. He has recently finished his first novel, *The Spot* (yet unpublished) and is working on a second, *Wishing on the Moon*. Dennis lives in Robbinsville, New Jersey with his wife, Nancy.

Denita Stevens was born and raised in Texas, but now she resides in New Jersey with her beloved Pomeranian. She is the author of *Invisible Veils*, a collection of poems which gives insight into what it's like to live with anxiety, depression and survive the trauma of being sexually assaulted. Her next book will be her memoir, Disorderly Life, which is about how she spent more than a decade living with undiagnosed PTSD, but started to heal after finding the help she needed. Find out more at denitastevens.com

Hope Is the Lighthouse
By Denita Stevens

Time passes
Like sand steadily sliding
Down the neck of an hourglass

Our passage
On this planet
Goes according to plan

Whether it be our plan
Someone else's plan
Or God's plan

We're not always in control
Even though we're the captain
Of our own ship

We sail along
Living the life
We've chartered

Navigating through waters
At a placid pace
Until we encounter

Unwelcome and unexpected
Tumultuous territory
We swing and sway

With the sea
Being whipped
By the wind

Our journey
Our life
Becomes turbulent

Clouded by a storm
Threatening
To change our course

For better or for worse
We ride it out
Gripping the wheel

Hope is the lighthouse
During the darkest of days
Guiding our way

An award-winning songwriter, author, researcher and historian, **Dave Hart** is a descendant of a New Jersey Signer of the Declaration of Independence. He is a Trustee for the Trenton Historical Society and a life member of the Ewing Township Historic Preservation Society.

His recent publications, written with his long-time collaborator John Calu, include *TRENTON*, a historical novel and *ADVENTURES ALONG THE JERSEY SHORE*, featuring many myths, legends and everyday mysteries of the Garden State. For more information, check out the publisher's website at https://hartcalu.com/

Story 1

'Touched'

By Dave Hart

I have never been abducted by aliens and, from what I've heard, read about and seen on TV, I don't ever want to be.

Of course, I've seen strange lights in the sky I was unable to explain or identify. But by now, who hasn't? That doesn't mean it was a UFO in the extra-terrestrial sense. It just means I don't have a good explanation for what I saw.

But I have had a few otherwise profound paranormal experiences of the most unusual kind that I would like to share. Three in particular, all from deceased 'loved ones' in which the messages sent and entities conveying them, are in my opinion at least, all without a shred of doubt.

The first one was from my father-in-law, Bos Holland. It occurred in October 1980, the same year the Phillies won their first World Series. Following a massive a heart attack at work, his second, he was taken to the University of Pennsylvania for observation. That night, as I lay on my back sleeping restlessly, I suddenly felt this tremendous weight pressing down on my chest like an elephant was sitting on top of me. It literally knocked the wind out of me and left me gasping for breath. I dared not wake my wife for fear of frightening her to death for no apparent reason.

At six the following morning, my mother-in-law received a call from the hospital with word that Bos had taken a turn for the worse. The nurse insisted the family should come to the hospital right away. We all went together.

When we arrived, we were immediately informed my father-in-law was already gone, that he had, in fact, actually passed away during the night at around the same time as my elephant's visit. Intuitively, the message was clear to me. It wasn't an elephant I experienced. And it wasn't a dream. It was Bos. Having two daughters and no sons, my father-in-law had stopped by on his journey into the next world and, upon his departure, had passed on to me the paternal responsibility for the family. That was the 'weight' I felt that night. I hope I haven't let him down.

The next time occurred in 1996. It came from my mother, Mary, and to this day remains a cherished treasure because something so incredibly extraordinary happened. She was receiving experimental chemotherapy treatment for colon cancer that she'd developed at age seventy-three. After her treatments, she and I would frequently stop at the local diner for a bit of breakfast and enjoy a few precious moments of normalcy. She knew her condition was terminal but she soldiered on with the treatments anyway.

A die-hard Roman Catholic all her life despite the tremendous adversities she bore without complaint, during one conversation I asked her if she would somehow let me know after she passed on if what she believed in so ardently in this life through her deep, abiding faith in the Almighty was indeed waiting for her when she got to her final resting place beyond. She agreed readily. In fact, she almost seemed to welcome the idea, even anticipate it, and indicated without hesitation that her sign to me would be the appearance of a beautiful white dove, the universal symbol of purity and peace.

When mom passed away in March, for weeks afterward I searched the skies and the surrounding outdoor areas for signs of her precious white dove. Although I couldn't honestly remember ever seeing one in the wild before, I nevertheless purposefully took long walks alone along the Delaware-Raritan Canal near where I lived just to look for her signal. Alas, it was to no avail.

Then one night after work I received a telephone call from mom's former hospice nurse, Maureen Van Niel, asking to see me right away. She sounded excited but wouldn't let on what she wanted to tell me until she saw me in person. Maureen and my mother had formed a very warm and tender bond during their time together. Maureen, who was then with child, and mom often spent hours talking about the importance of family and all that it meant.

It was Maureen who was the first to arrive on the scene at my sister's home where mom was staying to pronounce my mother had slipped away in the night following what had been an extremely peaceful vigil with all her family sitting around her bedside. Afterward, I briefly told Maureen about my mother's promise to me.

So, it was now several months later while servicing another grieving family in her hospice capacity that Maureen was presented with a gift from the deceased woman's husband. He claimed to have been 'directed' by his deceased wife to their china cabinet whereupon he proceeded to pull out and hand over to Maureen a white ceramic dove, saying, "This is for you. You'll know what to do with it!"

Indeed she did. Hence, her excited call to me. Leave it to my blessed mother to choose a most unusual and profound way to 'guide' her symbol of serenity through the hands of her dear hospice nurse on to her 'favorite' son completing the promise she had made to me. Message received, mom. It was unbelievable, proving beyond a shadow of a doubt that true faith has no bounds. Mom had made it to the Promised Land and it was, indeed, exactly as she had envisioned it. My heart leapt with joy at the confirmation. It still does. I know she is in good hands and at perpetual peace.

The third event came following the untimely death of my beloved wife of thirty-two years. Helaine had fought valiantly for more than a decade, overcoming three primary cancer diagnoses, two breasts and one ovarian, and the numerous surgeries, treatments and anxieties that came with them, all while continuing in her professional role counseling students at Trenton Central High School and administering to the endless demands of family. Now, however, due to the mega toxic levels of chemotherapy poured into her system over the those long, arduous years, she became afflicted with myelodysplasia, a severe pre-leukemic blood disorder that robbed her bone marrow's ability to create new white blood cells that were so desperately needed to fight infections. That was more than her poor, battered body could bear. She eventually succumbed to an unchecked infection acquired while hospitalized in the days immediately following a rushed colostomy, on of all days ... 9/11.

During the afternoon following her funeral service, as our daughter Michelle and I sat together in stunned silence on the couch in our once fun-filled family room, the framed classic white picket fence picture proclaiming, 'God Bless Our Home', that Helaine had cross-stitched decades earlier, suddenly fell from its revered place over our fireplace where it had hung undisturbed for the twenty-three years we had lived in the home.

It was early afternoon on a calm September day. Father and daughter were there alone. All the doors were closed. Not a window stood open. The central AC was off for the season. There was absolutely no other earthly reason for a disturbance of any kind to occur in that room.

After a long moment, Michelle and I turned to each other and uttered the same exact words: "Mom's here!" and indeed she was telling us in her not so subtle way that 'we we're still a family, that

31

this was 'still *our* home' and that I'll be 'with you always... love Mom.'

These are but a few of the many wondrous gifts that have been granted to me over the years for which I feel humbly blessed. There is a reality beyond this visible world trying to connect with us constantly. Everyday people are being 'touched' by loved ones who have crossed over and whose presence is there to be felt.

Now, I am just an ordinary person. I possess no special psychic powers and I am certainly not clairvoyant by any stretch of the imagination. I do, however, maintain an open and inquisitive mind. I am receptive to the possibilities beyond the veil of this life and try not to let the vicissitudes of the every day world get in the way of my receiving the many remarkable insights that can be glimpsed by all. Believe it! Someone may just be trying to get in touch with you!

Pearl Kennedy was born on May 29, 1950 in Greenock, Scotland. She met her husband, Dennis, in 1966 while he was stationed in her home town when he was in the US Navy, eventually moving with him to the United States. They married on September 8, 1967. She has five wonderful children, including her beautiful sunshine boy, Andrew, and she has ten grandchildren and two great grandchildren (with one more on the way). Pearl is currently a member at Cornerstone Bible Church in Port Jefferson Station, NY, where she works with the youth in Children's Church and Olympians. She is happy to share her and her husband's story in the hopes it will comfort and inspire those who have suffered from tragedy and are looking for peace beyond all understanding. (Philippians 4:7).

Story 2

Overcomer in Christ

By Pearl Kennedy

There are moments in life that define you. Moments where you have the choice of letting bad times overcome and control you or fighting back against the pain and turning a tragedy into a victory for Christ. This is a story of my husband, Dennis, who did just that.

It started off as a normal day in June. The children and I were in the kitchen baking strawberry shortcake to enjoy after my oldest son's baseball game that evening. Amid the flurry of baking and preparation for the game, my husband came home with a booming greeting, "How's my favorite family?" All was well until my oldest stumbled into the room with an ashen face and a dripping bundle in his arms...Andrew, my son...My sunshine boy. Not yet four years old... and not breathing. I screamed in terror as my husband lowered him to the floor and began CPR. The pool. He had fallen into the pool. Neighbors heard the frenzied screams of my other children and took them away, but I did not move. I could not. I stood frozen while my husband tried to get my son breathing again. Time blurred as they loaded my beautiful baby boy into an ambulance and rushed him to the hospital. They worked on him through the night, the longest night of my family's life. They placed him on a ventilator to aid his breathing. As dawn broke, we received news they had removed the ventilator… our baby boy was breathing on his own. The relief we felt, however, soon turned to devastation and despair as we were informed our sunshine boy was fading fast. He passed away in both our arms and into the arms of Jesus. As pained and numb as I was, I knew where my son was. My husband, unfortunately, did not.

Travelling to work each day, Dennis kept asking, "Why did he die?" He couldn't understand why God would want a little three year old. We both knew our lives would never be the same. Our hearts were broken in so many pieces, shattered beyond recognition. When I returned home the day of the funeral, I had no sense of motivation or purpose. I sat on the top of the stairs, motionless, for hours on end.

Dennis went off to work crying every day. He had no choice about work, he had to support the family. We struggled through, knowing our four other children were hurting. It was so traumatic for our oldest son, he was the one who found Andrew in the pool. Our oldest daughter was also brokenhearted. Because of their age, the two youngest didn't fully understand, but they knew something was wrong. They saw their dad and I crying all the time.

Being raised in a Born Again family, for as long as I can remember, I have always had the assurance of Heaven. When my sunshine boy took his last breath, he immediately fell into the arms of Jesus. My faith was the only thing to comfort me in those early days when all seemed lost and I was utterly without direction. I felt my heart break and my life over when we buried our son. I have never experienced that kind of pain before. I was so devastated. I did not know where to go or what to do. As the days passed, the pain was beyond severe, but I realized there were our four other children to care for. Despite my grief, I knew I must remain grounded and faithful for them. The realization made me more motivated than ever to teach my children about God's love for them.

My husband searched for two years, yearning to find answers. "Where is our son?" he would cry. I knew, but he did not. He searched and searched, he asked questions, but got no answers. His heart was too broken and too hardened. I came back to the Lord at this time and planted my feet on solid ground. My husband took a different road. He started drinking, trying to numb away the pain, fear, doubt and hurt. One day, in a wild rage, he tore through our home, destroying everything he touched. I still remember the sickening thud of our family Bible as it hit the wall, followed by his agonized scream, "How can I open my heart to Jesus when it's broken in pieces? How will there ever be a victory for Christ in the loss of my son?"

I continued to walk with the Lord, still asking Dennis to come to church. I knew he needed to accept Jesus Christ. He needed a peace from his sadness and pain that only God could provide. He was so torn, not knowing which way to turn. He was angry all the time, making all kinds of excuses not to join me and the children at church, yet I kept on praying. You see, I was still hurting inside, but I kept the Lord on my side. My poor, lost husband did not. Our children would come home from church saying, "Daddy, Jesus loves you."

Then one day, my soulmate said *yes,* I will go with you. After the service, he sat in our living room, processing what he had heard and felt. He mentioned how beautiful the hymns were, how they spoke of Jesus and how he felt as if the Pastor was talking to him personally about Christ and the sacrifice He made on the cross for all our sins. He told me, with tears forming in the corners of his eyes, the Pastor quoted a verse that touched his heart, John 3:16. *"For God so loved the world that He gave His only begotten Son, that whosoever believeth in Him should not perish, but have everlasting life."*

Then my sad, broken and angry soulmate turned to me, explaining how, as he sat in that little church listening to the songs and the Psalms, he realized something. God had a Son and lost Him, just like we had lost our baby boy. I hugged my husband tightly, whispering, "Thank you, Lord! Oh, thank you, Lord!" over and over again as I witnessed a thaw begin to spread in my soulmate's frozen heart.

During the next few weeks, my husband thought about what the Pastor had said. I began to see a subtle change in him and knew our lives were about to be transformed. Soon after, the Pastor and his wife came to visit. That time it was different. Dennis was taking in all the Pastor had to say, as he explained a person has to know Jesus as their Lord and personal Savior. At that moment, everything changed. My husband knew then Jesus was knocking on the door of his heart and he had either to reject Him or accept Him as his Lord. On that wonderful day in 1982, he got on his knees, tears flowing from his eyes, and became changed forever. He took Jesus into his heart. He changed his life, changed mine and changed our family's lives.

All these years later, I can look back on the agony and the tragedy we have borne and can honestly say it has been a wonderful victory. I know, through the scriptures, my little son is safe in the arms of Jesus. "One day," my husband said, just as King Davis said when losing his son, "I will go to him, but he can never come back to me."

It's been three years now since my soulmate, my husband Dennis, made his journey to his eternal home. I still cry, asking the Lord to hold me while I mourn. We were married just shy of 50 years and I am sad to be here without him. I will always love him. On the harder days, I comfort myself by singing *Until We Meet Again*. I remind myself often of this beautiful man and the many ways he showed God's love. When people tried to knock his faith, he stood firm. He was a very special man who made the world better for those who knew him I am proud and honored by the beautiful legacy he left behind.

I can say with assurance my Christian life has been wonderful in Jesus. Service for Him is service for an eternity. I wish for you all, if you don't know Jesus as your Lord and Savior, you would get on your knees like my family did. You will be forever changed.

1 Corinthians 15:3-4 *"For I delivered unto you first of all that which I also received, how Christ died for our sins according to the scriptures; And that He was buried, and that He rose again the third day according to the scriptures."* The Gospel of the Lord Jesus Christ. Make Jesus Christ your personal Savior today. God Bless you all.

"Dame" Dr. Gilda Battaglia Rorro Baldassari is a former model/actress in Mexico, an award-winning television teacher, educator/administrator, author, and civil rights leader. She represented the country of Italy for 20-years as Honorary Vice Consul for Italy, in Trenton, and as a Consular Correspondent.

Dr. Battaglia Rorro Baldassari initiated several 'Sister City' relationships between Italy and New Jersey, as well as an educational exchange program with schools in Haiti and the Garden State. As a former Chair of the New Jersey Italian Heritage Commission, she spearheaded the development of 'The Universality of Italian Heritage' curriculum--a series of 60 educational lessons to integrate Italian cultural heritage in all school curricula K-12.

She received lifetime achievement awards for her work in education and the Jefferson Award from the United States Senate for lifetime achievement in voluntary service.

She was knighted by the president of Italy.

Story 3
THE BRIDGE

By Cav. Gilda Battaglia Rorro Baldassari, Ed.D.

I was sitting in the back seat of our new Volvo as my son, Michael drove my husband, Louie, and me to JFK Airport. It was a splendid, sun-filled Sunday in January 1990. Cellina, a cousin through marriage, had invited me to her villa in Trani after Mom died two weeks before. I felt close to Cellina since we first met in 1951, in the seaside town of Margherita Di Savoia, where Dad was born. Her presence in my life has always been a special gift.

"Gilda, come to my home and stay as long as you like. You must get away from all your responsibilities and the sadness of your dear mother's passing."

Cellina's right. I'm exhausted from Mom's battle with colon cancer and miss her so much.

My mind wandered to the night before Mom died at Saint Francis Hospital, where she said, "Gilly, my mother is here. She came to protect me from danger."

My mother's countenance seemed different; she was uncommonly peaceful.

"She is by the door, smiling, in a red cowl neck blouse. Her hair is in a bun and she is wearing her favorite blue cameo necklace and earrings that I gave her."

"Does Grandmom know I'm here?

"Yes, she does, and she's smiling."

"Please tell Grandmom that I love her very much."

"She already knows, Gilly."

It was beautiful to hear and something I will always remember: that loved ones in heaven feel our presence and watch over us. My sadness at my mother's imminent passing was eased by her vision and belief that Grandmom would soon usher her to the 'other side'.

As we rode on the highway, I contemplated being in Italy for a ten-day visit. Louie could not leave his medical practice and my children had to stay behind to attend school. I would miss them, since they normally would come with me.

My new pink American Tourister suitcase took up a large space on the floor, leaning against the back seat. Glancing at it, a troubling thought came to mind.

If there were an accident, I should hold on to that luggage for support.

Annoyed with myself for letting a dark thought invade the bright sunlight, I was also aware that my long, looped, clip-on metal earring felt too tight. It was annoying, but I did not bother to adjust it.

"We're coming close to the Outer Bridge Crossing," Louie announced.

Gazing below at the blue expanse of the Arthur Kill Tidal Strait soothed my mind.

I love the water. This time tomorrow, I will be basking in the Adriatic Sea--shimmering and serene, melding with the azure sky.

Soon, we approached and ascended the bridge.

"Oh, no!" Michael exclaimed in a panic-filled voice.

"What's the...?" But before I could finish my question, an explosive sound erupted. A tractor trailer rear ended our Volvo,

44

sending it into a tailspin. The impact thrust us forward and sideways, sending us crashing into the guard rail.

Dear Lord, we might go over the barrier and plunge into the water.

Terrified, I clung to the heavy luggage with my eyes closed as our vehicle swerved, ramming into the auto ahead. That car and ours continued to collide into other vehicles, which simultaneously turned and struck both our passenger doors amid relentless, deafening noise.

The Volvo came to a screeching halt at the crest of the bridge. Multiple police cars and an ambulance arrived in a blaring cacophony of sirens.

An officer told Michael and Louie to exit quickly, leaving me trapped alone in the cream-colored interior of our white auto. The driver's seat in front of me had collapsed, pinning me down in the rear, next to the pink suitcase.

"Move that truck off that car NOW!" an officer shouted in a stentorious voice.

Turning my head, I gasped. The rear window was enveloped by a mountain of white. The front of the 24-ton trailer had climbed up our trunk, mooring it to the ground. Slowly, a crunching, scraping sound heralded the removal of the behemoth. Unable to move from my cramped space, I noticed my clip-on earring lay on the floor, beside the brake pedal.

Look at that! The impact was so great, my tight, right earring blew off to the front of the car.

While I reached to feel if the other one was intact, a greater horror began to unfold. Sitting helpless in the back seat, I fixated on the bare steering wheel of the driverless Volvo, which appeared to be propelled by a ghost. The car began to descend the inclined lane of the bridge.

This is surreal-- like an Alfred Hitchcock movie. The bridge has turned into a roller coaster. I am unable to move. The car is careening downward and will soon roll over. I am helpless to stop it. The collisions didn't kill me, but this will.

My mouth contorted into a silent scream. I wanted to say goodbye to my family, or utter a prayer when I saw a man running at top speed toward the car. He was of medium build, wearing a dark brown suit and tie. He somehow managed to fling open our driver's side door and engage the emergency brake.

This benevolent and heroic stranger saved me. This is not my day to die.

"Are you all right?" he asked, panting.

"Yes. Ah, I think so."

My rescuer walked me to the ambulance. I turned to look back at the heap of crumpled vehicles. In addition to the long trailer and our Volvo, five other cars had significant damage.

"Sit on this bench and relax with the gentleman who stopped your car. I need to examine you for injuries," the paramedic said. "Luckily, there were no fatalities. Your husband and son are shaken, but unharmed. Everyone involved needs X-Rays, and to be examined for soft-tissue injuries. You must go to a hospital now."

My rescuer turned to me.

"How do you feel?" he asked.

"Numb."

Still in a state of shock, I did not look at him directly. Instead, my eyes remained fixed on the floor. The sound of his soft voice was reassuring.

"Let me introduce myself. I'm Dr. Levine. I'm a cardiologist. Your car struck mine first. Someone told me you were headed for JFK for a trip to Italy. You must be very disappointed that you must postpone your travel plans, but if someone showed me your car and told me you walked out of it alive without a scratch, I would never believe it. Madam, consider this the luckiest day of your life!"

"Thank you, doctor. I feel truly blessed that you ran to my aid. You did your mitzvah and saved my life. How can I ever repay you?"

"You are here, safe and sound. There is nothing more I want."

Reflecting on his words, gratitude enveloped me.

He's right. I am incredibly fortunate to be alive. Because of this extraordinary "Good Samaritan," I will live to see another day. Was it luck or was this kind stranger an angel sent from Mom and Grandmom?

Looking heavenward, I said: "Thanks, Mom."

Kristin Perilli was born in Princeton, NJ and raised in a Catholic home in Hamilton Square, NJ. She is married to Bill Perilli and has four beautiful children: Andrew, Christian, Ryan and Gianna. She has her Master's Degree in occupational therapy from the University of Scranton. She began her career in Washington, DC working with active duty military personnel suffering head injuries from the Iraq and Afghanistan wars. She now stays home to raise her children. She enjoys occasional consulting work and being involved with her children's school, St. Gregory the Great Academy.

Story 4
Saint Gianna

By Kristin Perilli

In the midst of my suffering, it was hard for me to see the miracles unfolding in my life.

I wasn't expected to have children. Due to menstruating only one to two times a year, multiple cysts on my ovaries and an autoimmune thyroid disorder, I was told to prepare for adoption.

Shortly after I married my husband, Bill, we conceived Andrew. After his birth, the doctor congratulated me, but told me I may still need to prepare for adoption, given my ovaries were covered in cysts. This first C-section left me with an 8-inch separation in my abdominal wall. My organs protruded, giving the appearance I was five months pregnant. Even worse, caring for my child was a daily struggle. Living with chronic pain wasn't something I handled well. As a new mom on no sleep and chronic pain, I felt isolated and discouraged.

However, I became encouraged by my aunt who told me she was praying for me at the St. Gianna shrine. I knew nothing of St. Gianna. Many people began telling me to pray to her to conceive more children, as she is the patron saint of mothers and unborn children. As a busy new mom, I intended to pray to her and to look up her information, but, quite honestly, never did. Little did I know she would keep showing up in my life.

During a move from Bethesda, Maryland to New Jersey, I came upon a St. Gianna medal, which had been gifted to Andrew after he was born. A few months later, I lectured at mass where a large picture of St. Gianna was positioned on the altar next to the

49

pulpit. I felt as if I was being reminded of her wherever I went. Finally, I took the time to research the meaning of St. Gianna.

I discovered there is a St. Gianna fertility clinic in New Jersey that treats women with the exact condition I have. At that moment, I felt an overwhelming belief God was guiding me through the intercession of St. Gianna. I called the clinic to make an appointment, only to find out, shortly thereafter, I was actually pregnant. Until that point, every doctor told me that would be difficult to impossible.

My first prenatal appointment confirmed I was, indeed, pregnant with my second son Christian, and quite surprisingly, my ovarian cysts were gone. I was amazed and grateful. However, my abdomen worsened during that pregnancy, causing me much more pain. Following Christian's birth, St. Gianna came to me again in the form of a Christmas card from a friend from college. It was so nice to see photos of her beautiful growing family because we hadn't spoken in years. I cried immediately. As I opened the card, a relic of St. Gianna fell out. At that moment, I knew St. Gianna's intercession was how I was able to conceive children.

It became so clear to me my suffering was a way to bring me closer to Jesus. It was my calling to have more faith in His will for my life. In some ways, it was difficult. I like to be in control. I am a first-born child. I like to plan, organize, have a routine and structure. I like to be proactive and know what's coming along my path. God was slowly teaching me I needed to let go and allow Him to manage my life. My chronic pain turned out to be a blessing, as it served as a reminder to always pray to Him and to offer up each daily task as acknowledgment, He can help me through my day. I needed His strength because I could not rely on my own. Overall, I needed to trust. More specifically, to trust He was in control of my life, my children, my marriage and even my pain. There is something freeing in letting go and trusting Him.

Two years after the birth of my second son, I was blessed with a third son, Ryan. As happy as I was, my faith continued to be tried as my stomach pain increased. At that point, the fascia holding what was left of my abdominal wall was just about tearing. Tying shoes, changing diapers, cooking, cleaning and picking up children were all simple but terribly painful activities. I did my best to offer up my suffering. I learned more about St. Gianna and began to understand why she revealed herself to me. She suffered terribly during the pregnancy of her 4th child, dying in childbirth for the sake of saving her child. I prayed - St. Gianna, you understand what it feels like to suffer for your children. Please help me endure this for the sake of my children.

I consulted with a plastic surgeon who told me I needed surgery immediately. He described the surgery as something I would never want to go through again, so having more children was out of the question. He also didn't know if my skin could even hold another child inside my body. My husband and I agreed we needed to move forward with the surgery.

After several hours, my abdominal wall was re-approximated with a couple hundred stitches, my organs were back in the right places and I began my recovery. The doctor was right. I never wanted to go through that surgery ever again. The three C-sections didn't even come close to the pain after that surgery. I did need one repair after the initial surgery and had a hard time recovering. The nausea from the antibiotics and the fatigue from yet another surgery were absolutely debilitating. My husband worked long hours in New York City and I found myself counting down the minutes until he came home. I let go and surrendered to the help of family and friends. The meals, babysitting and care were humbling. I was used to doing it all on my own. God was reminding me these children actually belong to Him. They are mine only for a short while on this Earth and I needed to allow others to help me care for them.

I soon discovered the debilitating nausea and fatigue were because I was pregnant. This time, I was terrified. I immediately called my plastic surgeon. He wasn't sure what would happen to the fresh stitches. He also said he didn't know what to expect as the baby grew. The general surgeon agreed, she didn't know what to expect. She didn't know anyone who had gotten pregnant after that type of surgery. I was told I may experience a lot of pain, but pain medication wouldn't be wise to take while pregnant. In tears, I called my Ob-Gyn, a man of great faith, which showed in the manner with which he responded to my call. He agreed with the surgeons but said, "Don't worry, you will be ok. Given the circumstances, there is a reason for this baby and you will be just fine."

That pregnancy was the most difficult. The surgeons did such a great job of rebuilding my abdominal wall that it didn't want to stretch as the baby grew. I could feel the constant pull of the stitches. Since I wasn't stretching outward, the baby grew up underneath my rib cage, feeling like it was in between my legs. That's the only way I can describe it. I couldn't breathe. I couldn't eat. I couldn't move well. The baby was putting pressure on my stomach, so any food that entered my stomach would literally be kicked out by the baby. I cried a lot. I prayed a lot. I begged God to take the pain away, but it got worse as the pregnancy progressed.

During a routine ultrasound, I discovered the baby's growth slowed significantly. They had to do a C-section that day. We were warned the baby could have complications for being early and the C-section may be longer than my others, given my surgical history.

Gianna Denise was born on June 21, 2017 and was absolutely perfect. We experienced no complications and my recovery was the easiest of all my childbirths. She is absolutely beautiful and such a gift.

Looking back, those years were filled with miracle after miracle. Of course, my children are the biggest miracles of them all. However, I consider my physicians, the babysitters, the home cooked meals and prayers all miracles along the way.

On the days I am overwhelmed by motherhood, I am reminded of the patron Saint of Mothers, St. Gianna, and that my vocation is the greatest gift of all. Trust in Him. Trust His will and let go of what you think life should be like. Allow God, with all the angels and saints, to work miracles in your life.

Christine O'Shea resides in Naples, Florida with her mate of 25 years, plus her buddy Rocky, an Old English Sheepdog. Rocky is a rescue dog adopted from the Old English Rescue of South Florida. Christine loves animals and volunteers in the Naples Humane Society, serving as a 'Feline Ambassador'.

Prior to moving to Naples, Christine lived on a Horse Farm in Hopewell, New Jersey. She holds a Graduate Certificate from Rutgers University in Equine Management.

In 1994, Christine became a licensed Real Estate Salesperson in New Jersey, and in her first year, received the President's Club Award from Re/Max for sales excellence.

Besides the love of animals, Christine puts her 25 years of experience helping people achieve their Real Estate Goals and also holds a Real Estate Brokers License in Florida.

Story 5

TAKE ME WHERE YOU WANT ME TO GO

By Christine O'Shea

We will always remember 9/11/01, where we were and what we were doing at the precise time each of us learned our country was under attack. I will never forget that day when the Twin Towers came down. It felt like the world was coming to an end.

Early that morning, I had called the receptionist looking for a Fed Ex envelope. "It's not here yet," she replied. "Did you hear what happened in New York?"

Being a slow morning-person and not a fan of morning news, I had no idea what she was about to tell Maurice and me. Maurice, my significant other for 7 years, was a Real Estate Broker. I was a Sales Associate. We were dumbfounded. Turning on the TV, we watched in horror as the second plane crashed into the other Tower.

Later, during the drive up Route 1 to our Carnegie Center office in Princeton, New Jersey became surreal. Traffic was light and the parking lot was nearly empty.

"It is a beautiful crisp fall day, how could this be happening?" I remember asking Maurice, who was at a loss for words.

I hurried into the office, made a few phone calls, checked email, retrieved my Fed Ex package and left. We stopped for lunch at a local restaurant, which was nearly empty. Those there were somber, staring at the news broadcast on TV.

Later that night, sitting outside in our hot tub, I noticed there was not a plane in the sky. The stars were bright, the world was standing still, in shock and in mourning.

I was scheduled for outpatient surgery the following week. The Friday afternoon after the attack, I went for my pre-op testing at Princeton Medical Center. On the way home, I stopped at St. Paul's Roman Catholic Church, located on Nassau Street in downtown Princeton. I felt a strong urge to be around others and to pray in a church.

A few years earlier, I had gone into the same church with my mother and her friend, who were both visiting me. We each said a prayer and lit a candle. They explained it was a tradition to light a candle in a church you had never been to before.

On that Friday, upon entering during the middle of the sermon, I noticed the church was packed. The priest was recounting the events of September 11th and told the story of Father Mychal Judge, a Franciscan friar and Chaplain for the New York City Fire Department.

Father Mychal, one of the first responders, had lost his life, being hit by falling debris while in the Twin Towers. The service was very emotional. I took communion for the first time in a very long while. During the weeks to come on the news, I would see the famous photo of Father Mychal being carried from the rubble of the Twin Towers.

I still have fleeting memories of the days and weeks that followed. I recall worrying about one of my clients who worked in New York City (I later heard he was okay). I remember going past the Princeton Junction train station that week. All was quiet. There were cars parked that had not moved, the owners never having returned from the city that fateful and horrible day.

Stories were broadcast about victims and their loved ones. Vigils and prayers became commonplace. Scenes of flower tributes and photos of missing loved ones filled the screens of the nation's TVs. So sad. It hurt my heart and soul. It hurt everyone.

Life and our country were never the same. Days went by, turning into weeks and months, then years. Life as we knew it changed but continued.

Sometime around 2008

New Jersey winters became too harsh for us. Ice and snow were not our friends and Maurice and I headed south to Naples, Florida. We moved into a somewhat smaller and older golf club community, falling in love with the lush and mature landscaping. I now refer to it, however, as 'Crooked Brook'. There were 'red flags' regarding this particular community of which we should have taken heed, but we chose to ignore them.

We had attended an open house where an agent showed us the home in which we were interested. The prices in that area were low compared to neighboring communities. The Homeowner's Association fees and the Club fees were high, we were told, to keep out the 'riff-raff'.

Our agent lived and worked in the community, as did his very enthusiastic partner. The house we wanted had been on the market for more than four years and we were able to negotiate a very low price. The owner wanted OUT!

In an unusually short period of time, we were approved by the Club Board and Home Owners Association, the title work and inspections were finished, closing was accomplished and we were able to move in quickly. This became our long-term home, a place to settle in, work and relax. It did not take us long to realize, however, we had made a severe error in judgment.

The majority of residents in that community, who were older than us, had been taken advantage of by the Crooked Brook Bullies. Bullies come in all shapes and sizes. These unfortunate residents had collected their golden parachutes from their corporate positions and moved into what eventually became referred to as 'Heaven's Waiting Room', birthing the saying among residents, "You buy here, you die here!" What we considered sarcasm was, in reality, fact.

Our paradise and long-term home was going to become our living hell.

Soon after moving in, we received our Broker's Licenses and placed our focus on 'Crooked Brook', determined to make a difference, to make things better. We planned to market those stalled properties.

Another couple living in the community, both Sales Agents and considered the 'go to' agents in Crooked Brook, consistently overpriced listings to kept them on the market for three, four or more years, eventually wearing down the sellers to sell for a below market price.

We began taking the over-priced, expired listings of the other two agents to list and place them under contract in a matter of days. The residents loved it.

The Club and Association Bullies were devious. Constant assessments, along with increased dues, were placed on the homeowners. Club membership was mandatory, with a large equity fee to live in the community. Every year, there was a new fee, each year being raised significantly, as were Association dues.

2014-2015

The community was faced with another assessment, a rather large one, for a new pool and fitness center, charging each homeowner over $10,000. Some wanted it while others, including us, did not. A battle ensued. Once again, we were on the opposite side of the other two agents. We outlined why there should not be an assessment or a tear down of the pool and fitness center, but instead, a refurbishing of that facility. We rallied for a NO vote.

Those who wanted this assessment held meetings, insisting on their view. There seemed to be much more to it than just an assessment and a new fitness center. The large sum of money being demanded was needed for something, the question was what?

During this time, we became members of the Catholic Church on Marco Island. Maurice joined the Knights of Columbus and it did not take long for him to become a 4th Degree Knight. My heart sang for joy as we attended mass every Sunday.

Spiritually, I was in a good place. I was filled with faith and gratitude. Meanwhile, things in Crooked Brook were starting to boil over. The community became divided between those who wanted the assessment and those who did not. Tensions rose. Opposing groups did not speak to one another.

We remained in the background, running silent opposition to the fitness center, sending emails from a web site created to 'Save Crooked Brook'. There was a chat page and emails. Things between opposing residents became UGLY.

The day of the vote came and the fitness center was voted DOWN. Sweet victory, a true win. The Bullies were defeated. Within a few months, the fitness center issue appeared again in another form. A new proposal and a new assessment.

Around that same time, underhanded gossip and lies surfaced throughout Crooked Brook regarding our business practices. It was retaliation by the Bullies for our part in voting down the fitness center and taking business from the other two sales people.

We were threatened and harassed in ways I cannot write about. The situation became unbearable for me. I could no longer live like that. My relationship with Maurice fell into serious trouble. I blamed him for the situation, for insisting we live in Crooked

Brook. I blamed him for focusing on doing business in Crooked Brook and for fighting with the Bullies.

My health and well-being were on edge. I could not sleep, worrying someone was going to hurt me. I packed my possessions and left to stay with my mother. When Maurice asked me when I was returning, I told him I did not know. In my mind, I said never.

Once at my mother's, I refused to speak with him. The weeks passed and I settled down, putting my life into perspective. Maurice and I slowly began communicating.

One night, I received a text from Maurice. "Something happened. I need to tell you about it."

When I called him later that night, I could tell his voice was choked up.

"It was amazing," he said. "I went to the Knights of Columbus meeting, where I asked for prayers for you and for your mom. After the meeting, a man approached me, someone I had never seen there before. He told me I looked troubled and he wanted to share something with me, to pray with me. He said he had a very special item, a New York Fire Department badge in a leather case that belonged to the fallen priest, Mychal Judge. He placed it in my hand and covered his hand on top of mine. He explained how some people feel a burning while other people feel something different, a fluttering of their heart."

"Go on," I urged him. "Tell me more."

Maurice continued, "He and I started to pray…I felt a burning on my hand, it was like nothing I had ever felt, like a hot coal…it was incredible, it was scary."

"What happened next?" I asked.

"He gave me a prayer card and walked away."

That card read as follows:

Lord, take me where you want me to go.
Let me meet who you want me to meet.
Tell me what you want me to say
And keep me out of your way.

Maurice told me, after that encounter, he just sat in the car for some time, thinking and reflecting. What he explained as a scary experience, I considered to be the Holy Spirit speaking to him through this random person no one at the meeting seemed to know. Someone who had not been seen since that evening.

I remembered Father Mychal. I told Maurice I believed his contact with that man was truly a divine intervention.

Since that time, every morning before he puts his feet on the floor, the prayer from that card is said then repeated through the day. When he meets people and a spiritual discussion ensues, he shares the story, the prayer and the prayer card, if he happened to have one on hand.

That was the start of our reconciliation, of our getting back together and facing our challenges again.

Life and relationships are not always easy. Sometimes, one has to swallow pride to compromise and move forward.

Many challenges have been presented to both of us since that period in our lives over five years ago, but with Faith, Grace and the Mercy of our Lord, we carry on, handing it over to God to lead us where he wants us to go.

NOTE: There are some wonderful stories about Father Mychal Judge, one in particular on YouTube: 9/11 Remembrance - Remembering Father Mychal Judge.

Gina A. Di Iorio is an American clinical nutritionist, TV personality, lecturer on Holistic Health, forthcoming author, home health advocate, lifestyle expert, wife, speaker, mother and grandmother.

Over 36 years ago, Gina followed the Holistic model: body, mind, emotion and spirit. Using nutrition as a foundation for optimal health, Gina elevated her health by nurturing her body, a self-care practice she continually embraces by consuming GMO free nutritious, organic wholefoods for healthy living. She founded Holistic Nutritious Solutions, LLC, in 2016. Gina empowers individuals to make practical healthy choices when it comes to nutrition and lifestyle choices in order to build health on a daily basis. www.HolisticNSolutions.com

Gina has recently appeared on the CWPhilly Network Television show, *Unplugged with Eraldo*, and a guest on, *The Expert Channel*. Recently becoming a grandmother in 2018, she loves to play with her grandson Douglas. Gina enjoys traveling the world with her husband, Sam, on bike, on foot and in the air.

Story 6

Alignment with the Universe: Answered Prayer on an Airplane

Gina A. Di Iorio

Have you ever had an occurrence in your life that left you saying, "Wow! What a coincidence!" leaving you a bit awestruck? I have had several throughout the years, these so-called 'coincidences'.

Years ago, a friend of mine suggested a great read entitled *When God Winks*, by Squire Rushnell who, in it, coined the term 'Godwink'. The term referred to seemingly random events taking place of which you take notice, becoming aware of their coincidental nature.

After reading the book, with such events having transpired in my life, I gained a greater awareness of what I was creating between the powers of prayer and aligning my prayers out into the universe, having them connected to 'my universe'. These coincidences are the alignment with the universe Rushnell described in his book. This concept of a coincidence, or Godwink, really blew my mind.

An example of a personal Godwink came to bear after I opened my business, Holistic Nutritious Solutions, LLC, in 2016. At 50 years old, my passion for Holistic Health came into fruition. Being a new entrepreneur, I needed a suitable headshot for my website. I was searching for a photographer in the area, but was unable to connect with anyone. For several months, I used an amateur photo of myself, still wishing to connect with a photographer and his or her work that would utterly inspire me. Both had to give me the WOW Factor, something and someone that would stand out in the light. His or her works and passion, somehow, would need to resonate with me and leave me speechless.

65

I felt this way with one of my favorite photographers, always admiring his videos and photography, the late Herb Ritts. His works would take my breath away. One of his early works was a video he directed of Janet Jackson's *Love Will Never Do (Without You)*. Showing the symmetry of the body, both in color and in black and white, and the classic style of clothing left one unable to decipher the year the video was created. Janet wore a simple tank top and torn jeans. Being timeless with classical factors gave energy between the human touch and their connection. Nearly 30 years later, the video still stands the test of time; a prime example of the WOW Factor.

On April 18, 2017, I prayed out loud into the Universe, "I am looking for a great photographer and I not only want an awesome photo taken of myself but a connection in such a way I would be moved by both person and artistry." About five minutes after I uttered this prayer, I scrolled through Instagram and found a photo I really liked. I loved the Bohemian look of the model and how it was photographed in a natural setting. I went to the website and found some of the same quality of work I was searching for in a photographer. The name of the photographer was Debbie Gichan. Her work touched me in such a way, it stayed with me.

As weeks passed, I began preparing myself for a Health and Wellness Expo in Salt Lake City, and made a connection with Chris, a high school classmate I hadn't seen in years who resided in Utah. The result was fantastic. Though it had been 30 years since we last saw each other, Chris, his wife Katherine, my colleague and I enjoyed a night of laughter while dining out in a trendy restaurant.

On May 7, 2017, all packed and ready to return to New Jersey, I arrived at the Salt Lake City Airport, going through all the rigmarole of security and bag checks, only to find our flight was delayed. While waiting, I had the pleasure of meeting some of the Health and Wellness attendees of the Expo. We talked about how amazing the Expo was to have imbued us with essential information on health and wellness. At its big gala, dressed in our formal attire and meeting people from all over the world, was absolutely extraordinary. Sharing common goals of making a difference in health, and a positive impact on the environment, while assisting others to reach their goals enriched the occasion.

Upon finally boarding the plane, I felt so unbelievably blessed for the experience. My seat was in the aisle, with my colleague next to me and a woman we did not know in the window seat. Recalling the events of the health conference and seeing my former classmate and his wife, wonderful memories ran through my head. My body and mind felt so elated.

In the next few moments, I was about to find myself in a coincidence. The Universe was going to send a powerful message to me.

I always love to meet people and am very congenial. So, without hesitation, I introduced myself to the woman sitting in the window seat.

Low and behold, she responded, "My name is Debbie Gichan."

I nearly jumped out of my seat. My eyes grew wide with excitement. Wanting to be sure I heard her correctly, I asked, "Would you mind repeating your name?"

She repeated, "Debbie Gichan."

I excitedly gushed, "I think I'm following you on Instagram!"

Rustling in my purse for my phone, I was able to show her the Instagram account I was following.

"Is this you?" I asked.

"Yes, it is," she replied with a smile.

I could not believe it. I was in an airplane some 2,000 miles from home in Salt Lake City, Utah, sitting two seats away from a photographer I just started following on Instagram a few weeks ago.

My mind raced, "Gina, is this your answered prayer, two seats away in the physical form?"

What do I do next? Do I tell her the story of my prayer searching for a photographer? I felt compelled to do so and began telling my colleague and Debbie Gichan how I prayed and searched for a photographer.

Both their mouths dropped in awe, amazed with my story. None of us could believe the revelation taking place in that airplane and how the events of our individual lives connected at that very moment.

There is even more to this story of the universe aligning itself with me. Something more was about to take place during our meeting as we talked further. Still astonished at what had just taken place, I silently considered, "Is this the photographer I was praying for?" Her work on Instagram resonated with me but what about her story?" I urged myself, "Ask her more questions?"

I started with, "Where do you live?"

"Flemington, New Jersey - Raritan area," she answered.

I was struck again with amazement.

"Oh my God!" I blurted out. "I'm currently a co-host for two programs on a radio/podcast show in Flemington, *Awaken to Your Purpose* and *Living Consciously*. What a coincidence!"

My mind whirled, "Keep going Gina. There has got to be more to this woman. I must know her story and how I can continue toward another connection to her."

"I love your website and found your photos of the female subjects unique and ethereal. Very natural," I complimented with sincerity. "And I love the individual background you used for each of the photos too."

"Why thank you," she said. "What do you do?"

I told her I am a Clinical Nutritionist and spoke of the weekend conference my colleague and I attended.

"I'm a teacher and also a yoga instructor," she told us.

This was incredible! The three of us were involved in natural Holistic modalities. It was so amazing!   I kept urging myself, "Keep going Gina."

"How long have you been a yoga instructor?" I asked.

"Several years," she replied. "However, I started with ballet. During the course of studying ballet I was asked to take some photos, which started my passion for photography."

"I love how something we gain a passion for can open doors for other opportunities," I told her. "My uncle took up photography as a hobby and I loved being his subject when I was a little girl. I guess that's how I was introduced to the artful side of photography."

I mentioned how I had a few favorites, such as Richard Avedon and Herb Ritts, both so talented. I described how, being a Jersey Girl and a fan of Bon Jovi, I was aware Ritts had taken wonderful pictures of him and his family, as well as other celebrities.

"I just love his videos and photography," I explained. "His works of art really resonated with me."

As the revelation unfolded further, Debbie's next words astonished me, "I knew Herb. We attended the same school together."

The three of us laughed with incredulity as the connection gained another link.

I could not help but think, "That's it! I've heard enough! Gina, get her contact information!"

We exchanged our information and, happy to say, stayed in touch.

The flight could not have been more enjoyable. I could barely stand the excitement running through me. I had goose bumps all over my body. All three of us laughing, knowing this event made our day. I became certain I was on the right path, knowing I had found the right photographer to satisfy my requirements. Of all places to have an answer to a prayer come full circle, 2000 miles away from home on an airplane, I said to myself, "Praise the Lord! Thank you, God! I've gotten my own Godwink. I cannot believe it happened as it did!"

During that summer, I had the pleasure of having Debbie as a guest on both of my broadcasts, where we explained to our audience how we met. Even the host was left speechless hearing of the events leading to our connection.

On November 12, 2017, my 51st Birthday, Debbie took the photos I had long waited for. A few weeks later, she e-mailed them to me. Going through my headshots, I was immediately able to select the one I most connected to with great joy. Not only did it resonate with me, but it had the WOW factor. "This is the one!" I said aloud. I was thrilled.

A coincidence? No, a Godwink. My website received the headshot I wanted with an incredible story behind it. A powerful story that struck me with awe. I felt so unbelievably blessed by it. An awesome revelation of an answered prayer.

Something even bigger than ourselves is out there in the universe, listening, resonating with energy. We can connect with this power. A thought or a need can become prayer, sending it out to the universe.

As God/Universe, the source of this energy heard my call, ultimately manifesting itself into the physical, tangible substance entering into my reality, my universe.

Blessings to you as you pray. Soon, the God/Universe will align you on your path. Have faith. It can be revealed to you, taking place at anytime, anywhere, even on an airplane.

DJ Mickey G Entertainment, LLC is a full-service entertainment company offering an extensive menu of services. **Mickey Gordon** is our CEO/President. Mickey Gordon studied communications broadcasting and is Alum from Widener University. He has learned from some of the best and brightest professors and professionals in the field.

After graduating, Mickey was fortunate enough to take his entertainment career to the next level and become a top talent/personality for major radio (Clear Channel) and entertainment networks. Most notably Radio Disney and the Disney Channel. He has become one of the nation's top talents and most requested event/performance DJ and host. He has hosted/performed and opened shows for almost every celebrity artist in the business. He has an impressive following on social media and currently travels nationwide to perform for special events, concerts, private parties, school assemblies, universities and corporate affairs.

The last year to year and a half, Mickey has battled brain cancer and literally taught himself to do everything all over again. Despite his horrific struggle, he is back now and wowing audiences with his talents.

Story 7
Life's Direction
By Mickey Gordon

Life has a way of taking you in different directions when you least expect it. What makes the difference is how you respond. Do you go off the path and seek help, striving to do your best to heal? Or do you listen to what you're told?

I have defiantly been taken off the path, I have been totally lost.

Please allow me to introduce myself, I am Mickey Gordon, also known as DJ Mickey or DJ Mickey G. I have been behind the turntables since the age of 13. My passion began by DJ-ing for children with special needs. That progressed to DJ-ing for my fraternity on campus in college, major radio, television networks, and now, to doing two to four DJ events per day!

At the end of 2016 and the beginning of 2017, I started to experience horrid, debilitating vomiting for 3 months. Something was obviously not right. I visited six different doctors. Nobody could diagnose what was wrong with me. Thinking it was vertigo, since my equilibrium was also compromised, one therapist told me to go to an ENT (ear, nose, and throat) specialist. The specialist ordered an MRI with and without contrast.

In fear I would get sick during the MRI, I brought my throw up bowl with me… (I had to bring it everywhere).

The MRI revealed I had an undescribed tumor in my brain which measured at about 3 centimeters. It was suggested I seek help and go to the hospital right away.

A childhood friend of my wife recommended a doctor in Philadelphia. I went to his facility immediately. He told me what to expect with the surgery and the possible risks.

He told me: "You really need this surgery or you will become a vegetable." He also told me, "The surgery will be quick and painless."

Having a wife and boy/girl twins the age of two, I didn't want that to happen, so I agreed.

The doctor operated on my brain for 8.5 hours…. So much for a quick and painless outcome…. He sent my tumor out to the lab and it was unanimous I had cancer. It was called medulloblastoma. This type of cancer is only common in two percent of adults. I was in the lucky percent. This type of cancer is usually found in kids and teens.

I was told to combat this I would need radiation with proton therapy and chemotherapy. I had to have a spinal tap to see if the cancer spread to my spine. Thankfully nothing was found. The process was extremely painful. Two doctors had to stick me eight times before they got what they needed. I felt EVERYTHING….

After staying in the hospital for one week, I was moved to a rehabilitation hospital. I stayed there for three more weeks. A therapist worked with me while I was going back and forth to Philadelphia for tests and prep for what was to come.

During this time, I couldn't see well due to the massive swelling on the brain, my balance was horrible and my speech was drastically affected. I was confined to a wheel chair. I had to use a shower chair to sit and a hand/safety rail had to be installed in my home shower, so I wouldn't fall. I couldn't do much for myself at all. I needed help with everything.

I was told I would have a ten percent better chance of the cancer not coming back, if I have chemo on top of the vigorous radiation treatments. I'm by no means a mathematician, but since there wasn't any statistics on this type of cancer, as it's not common for adults, I respectfully declined.

I was determined to find another way...

"Never be afraid to try new things when you want to achieve your goals because you never know what can work for you."

The radiation treatments were a nightmare, from the dressing, to the setup, to the treatment itself. The side effects were similar to what chemo would have done. I threw up constantly, I lost all my hair and I felt extremely tired.

Needless to say, I wanted to die.

I begged my wife to kill me everyday. Of course, she wouldn't.

Honestly, I didn't have enough strength to do it myself....

Then I hit 'rock bottom', I was ready to give up hope of ever getting better.

I received a referral for acupuncture.... Having never had this done before, I didn't know what to expect. It would either work or not. Having nothing to lose, I gave it a shot. After the first treatment, I was amazed...I immediately noticed one of the symptoms went away. Giving me hope that something would work. After every visit, a symptom was either controlled or taken away. Little by little, every symptom was stripped away.

It took a full year of treatments. I wish someone would've told me it would take that long.

I'm convinced that acupuncture shaved some time off the healing process.

During the time it took to have every side effect controlled, I had to train myself how to do everything again.... Everything from seeing, speaking properly, driving myself, walking, dancing and going back to the gym to work out my usual 3 to 4 days a week to get strong. It took a while, but I'm alive, well, and symptom free!

People ask me, "How do you feel, Mickey"?

Up to this point I say, "I'm probably at ninety eight percent, I probably will never get the other two percent back but, honestly, the alterative could be much, much worse....

"Only weak people don't ask for help when they need it the most."

"Having good people to help you and stand by you, makes a huge difference."

"While you are going through cancer, your family goes through it too."

Life's GPS, while taking me through different turns and directions, finally found my destination to a healthier me!!

Mary Theresa Donegan-Weil is a former Irish Step Dancer who has danced at many venues including The Hibernians in Elizabeth, NJ, The Garden State Arts Center (currently PNC Bank Arts Center), but her proudest moment is when she performed at Carnegie Hall in NYC. Mary Theresa had one of the major roles in the play *The Fine Tapestry of Motherhood.* Involved with many Ministries at St. Gregory The Great Church in Hamilton, NJ, which includes singing Alto in the Choir, and Chair of The Golden Halo Ministry at St. Greg's along with her Golden Retriever Kimiko, a certified therapy dog, and many other dogs with their owners who bring emotional healing to children and adults in need of comfort through a visit.

Mary Theresa is a Real Estate Specialist located in N.J., who belonging to several multiple listing areas from North to South Jersey, who is passionate about helping each client go through a smooth transition.

Dedication

I dedicate this story to my dad, whom I miss every single day, and to my beautiful mom, Mary, who has always been our Irish Rock to me and my three sisters, Eileen, Noreen and Colleen. We have been through so much together, whether happy or sad, but our love and faith have always sustained us as a family. To my husband, Larry, and our son Thomas, thank you always for your love and support.

Story 8

Daddy

By Mary Theresa Donegan-Weil

My name is Mary Theresa. I write this on what would have been my dad's 90th Birthday.

It was a beautiful summer day in 1978 when parents of some of my high school friends took a group of kids on a road trip to Rockaway Beach, NY, singing and playing eye-spy along the way. When we arrived, the beach seemed very large and the water appeared calm and glistening. There were lots of children playing and swimming in the water so, of course, we couldn't wait to jump in, too…. and so, we did.

We were having so much fun until, all of a sudden, the lifeguards began whistling and yelling for everyone to get out of the water because the wave action was becoming more intense and the pull of the undertow was getting stronger. I remember being in the water, trying to hang on to one of my friend's brother, who thought I was joking so he pushed me away. It was not mean spirited, just kids being kids. He wasn't aware I needed help.

I felt the waves crashing over me and the undertow pulling me farther and farther away from shore. Feeling helpless, I held out my hand, yelling for help, not knowing if anyone saw or heard me. Suddenly, I stopped all movement, feeling a rush of peace and calmness come over me. My life flashed in front of me from when I was a little girl, like a running movie of my life. I found myself standing alone in a tunnel filled with the brightest beaming light. I remember, though the light was so intense, I could still look into it without turning away from the glare.

As I drew closer, the light seemed to dissipate and I could see two rows of family members of mine who had passed on. They were looking at me and smiling. I was so happy to see them. They stood erect like soldiers, facing each other with space between them, their heads turned towards me. I first noticed some of my aunts and uncles on the right side, then looked left and saw my dad. I was so happy to see him. He was smiling his familiar smile that could light up a room. As I gazed in awe, he said to me, "Don't worry. Everything will be all right." I thought to myself, everything is all right. I'm with my loved ones, especially my dad.

Right after my dad had spoken, I felt someone pulling me, then the surface water splashing my face. It was two lifeguards dragging me out of the water. They laid me on the sand next to an emergency vehicle that had driven onto the beach. They worked frantically to give me oxygen. As I opened my eyes, I discovered many on the beach had gathered around me. I spotted my friends and their parents and was touched they were crying. I had not yet realized how serious the situation actually was.

When I got finally up, my friends ran to me, amazed I had survived the ordeal. As the excitement ebbed, my friends went back in the water, but I didn't. I pretended to still be having fun, but deep down, I was nervous, somewhat embarrassed. The day at the beach finally came to an end. We packed our things and left for home.

Not long after, I began having dreams of rushing water. Whenever watching the introduction of the show Hawaii Five-0, I would gasp as if I needed air. I found I couldn't listen to the song *Rockaway Beach,* by the Ramones, without panicking. I had become profoundly affected by the event. Was it the near drowning, seeing my dad once more or both? I believed both, but which more so?

I resisted telling my mom of my experience involving my dad because of what had sorrowfully happened to him four years prior, fearing it would upset her terribly. I couldn't bring myself to do that to her, to have her re-live that awful time. It struck me with awe, however, that my dad was there to comfort me in my time of greatest need. That was my dad.

That sorrowful time I mentioned occurred just before Christmas, 1974, as we were happily preparing for the holiday, our house glistening with decorations, as did all the houses on the block. I remember, one evening, I was in the living room, my sisters were upstairs and my mother, Mary, was in the kitchen. My dad announced he was going out for a pack of cigarettes and would be back in a little while. Being a Sunday with the stores closed, the only place he could go was the Lamplight Inn, a pub within walking distance.

After a while, it had gotten late and my dad had not come home yet. We became worried. He hadn't taken his car, so he couldn't have gone far. We started to panic. My mom called my dad's brothers, Uncle Mike and Uncle Pat, who contacted the Lamplight Inn. The inn's bartender told them my dad had been there with a neighbor, but they had already left together. My mom rushed across the street to the neighbors', where she learned dad had stopped for a drink, had been in a good mood and was telling them how proud he was of his daughters.

As he was leaving their second-floor apartment, however, the stairway light was not on and he lost his footing, falling to the bottom. The neighbors called down asking if he was okay, to which he responded, "Yes, I'm fine." He left immediately thereafter, with the neighbors assuming he was alright.

With still no sign of him, a search was organized. His missing was announced on the TV and radio. His brothers, friends and co-workers searched for some time before deciding to look in Warinanco Park, a beautiful and serene park near our home with a large lake, where we all had rented row boats together.

The search continued for a few days to no avail until, one sunny afternoon, my dad's white shoes were seen floating on the surface. Soon after, they located my dad. My uncles brought my mother the sad news. My dad had been found; he had drowned.

It was never determined exactly what happened that night. It's believed he may have received a concussion from the fall, putting him in a confused state. Instead of simply walking across the street to our home, it was likely he walked around the corner into the park and stumbled into the freezing lake.

My poor mom was left alone to raise me and my sisters, Eileen and twins Noreen and Colleen. Being the oldest and in my freshman year at St. Mary's High School and with my mom working in St. Mary's Rectory as a cook for the priests, I was offered a job there, which helped with the family's expenses.

Back to the personal significance of the white shoes. My dad was a very handsome Irishman, born in Limerick, Ireland. With my mom being born in County Curry, Sligo, Ireland, Irish humor ran rapid in our home, which, along with our strong Faith in God, carried us through many ups and downs. Dad had such a great sense of humor, often telling his friends he looked like Tom Jones, with his wavy black hair, blue eyes and his very shiny white shoes, those very shoes found floating that terrible afternoon. I don't recall seeing the white shoes at Rockaway Beach, but it wouldn't surprise me if he was wearing them.

Years later, I finally did tell my mom what happened to me that day at the beach. When I told her Daddy was with me, telling me everything would be all right, it gave her great comfort. She was happy I got to see him and especially pleased to know he was fine and watching over all of us.

William Sheenan was born in Washington, D.C. and is the fifth of ten children. A member of a devout Catholic family, William was exposed early in life to the mysteries of his faith and participated in all facets of it during his youth, continuing throughout his life to present day. William is a member of the Lay Fraternity of Dominicans at his parish, St. Gregory the Great in Hamilton, NJ. He holds a Bachelor of Science (B.S.) in Agricultural Economics from The University of Maryland at College Park and an additional B.S. in Accounting from same. William is employed as a Helicopter Pilot with the U.S. Government. He is married and the father of three. He resides in Hamilton, NJ.

Story 9
The Miracle of the Two Hearts
By Bill Sheehan

My name is Bill Sheehan. In 1976, as an active five-year-old
boy growing up in the suburbs of Washington D.C., I began
displaying symptoms that were concerning to my mother. I tired
easily and my breathing grew rapid upon physical exertion.
Additionally, my fingertips and lips would turn blue when I ran
around in the yard. A visit to our family doctor confirmed there was,
indeed, something wrong with my heart. The doctor, Dr. Molling,
detected an abnormality and urged my mother to have me examined
by a Cardiologist at Children's Hospital in Washington, D.C.

The result of that examination was a diagnosis of Upper
Atrial Septum Defect, a condition allowing un-oxygenated blood to
flow from one atrial chamber of the heart into the other,
subsequently being pushed out into the body. While not an
immediately fatal diagnosis, if left uncorrected, would likely result in
an early death. Any operation to correct the problem would have to
be done before I reached puberty and require intrusive open heart
surgery. Joseph and Christina Sheehan, my parents, left the hospital
that day with the terrible realization their son would need open heart
surgery within five years. Our family doctor would monitor my
condition during those years.

My parents decided the best way to cure me was for the
entire family to devote themselves to The Sacred Heart of Jesus.
They did just that. They all prayed the Rosary for me every night,
went to First Friday Masses and prayed extensively to the Sacred
Heart of Jesus to heal me.

Five years passed. At the age of ten, my parents returned with
me to Children's Hospital for an assessment of my condition. I was
placed through a series of tests and x-rays, including a sonogram.
The doctors were confused with the results, telling my parents a
special x-ray was required for full verification, which I received. My

parents and I waited at the hospital for the results, which came quickly from the lead surgeon, who invited us into the tech area to view a series of x-rays lined up on an illuminated viewing screen.

The surgeon explained how the first few x-rays showed a perfect heart, free of any abnormalities, then drew our attention to the last x-ray, pointing to an anomaly just above the heart. It was the image of a cross, a fortuitous oversight by the x-ray technician, who had forgotten to remove it from my neck. The doctors were all amazed, remarking it appeared to them as Divine intervention, as there was no medical explanation for the heart's healing.

But the story continues...

Marty Sheehan, my younger brother by two years, was also diagnosed with the exact same condition in his heart, though his was much worse. Marty displayed many of the symptoms I had, resulting in our parents taking him to the heart specialist as well. Marty's diagnosis also came at about the age of five. When my heart had finally been healed, Marty was eight. My family hoped Marty's heart would follow the same course as mine and another miracle would bless the family. Like in my prognosis, only surgery would correct his condition and it had to occur before puberty. The next two years we would all pray fervently for another miracle.

Those two years passed. My parents took Marty to Children's Hospital for his evaluation. The findings were grim. Marty's heart had not healed. It was concluded he would need open heart surgery as soon as possible to correct the problem. That was a Friday afternoon. Marty and my folks were sent home with the instructions to return the following week to begin workups for Marty's pending surgery, which the doctors wanted to perform within the next few weeks.

My parents left the hospital with a revised plan of hope for a miracle. Pulling into a 7-11 Food Mart on the way home, my dad called a good friend named Father John Luby. Father Luby was very well known for being gifted with the power of healing. His rich history of incredible healings convinced our parents their calling him to bless Marty would be exactly what was needed to repair his heart. Father Luby responded by inviting them to come directly to his rectory in southern Maryland.

My parents and Marty did just that, driving straight from the 7-11 to Father Luby in Maryland. Upon arriving, they were met by Father Luby at the doorstep who, yet unaware of the full details of Marty's ailment, looked at him and said, "I am here to help fix your heart." He immediately invited them inside to discuss Marty and his ailing heart.

After being apprised of Marty's condition, Father Luby told my folks his gift of the Laying of the Hands was a very special one, explaining faith in Christ heals all. Father Luby asked Marty to sit next to him, then placed his hands on Marty's head, saying a quiet prayer with his eyes closed. Within a few moments, Father Luby opened his eyes and with a smile, claimed Marty's heart was healed. He explained he could tell in which instances God would grant a miracle because he would feel a vibration and warmth emanate from the person and from his own hands. He had felt these with Marty, thus knowing he was healed. My parents were then instructed to return to the hospital to have the doctors re-examine Marty's heart.

Joyous with the news, my parents did as instructed. Upon returning to the hospital the following week, they insisted another x-ray be taken of Marty's heart. When it was done, it confirmed his heart was 100% normal, without any defect. The doctor consulted with my folks, insisting, "I want the number of the Man upstairs who caused this to happen. You must have a direct line to Him. This was a miracle." In astonishment, he told them he could not think of an occasion where two brothers afflicted with the same condition were so completely healed without any medical intervention.

Before my father died at the age of 82 in 2017, he reminisced about his proudest moments in life, the greatest of which being a part of the two miracles of his sons' hearts.

My name is **Maria Remboski**. I am President of The Jeremy Fund, a non-profit organization raising money to help families of children with cancer. It is my desire to make a difference in the world. I am blessed with so many wonderful people in my life, like Paula Beiger, and I want to pay it forward by making a difference through helping others. I am a mother of four amazing children now and one beautiful angel in Heaven. My career is helping real estate agents achieve their dreams. I am the Team Leader of Keller Williams Premier, Robbinsville, NJ.

Story 10

Mommy, what do we do now?

By Maria Remboski

It was November 27, 1995, I think. That portion of time in my life is a bit of a blur. We had come home from Boston after a five-hour drive to a house filled with family, friends and Father Rich, our local priest. Everyone had gathered out of kindness, sadness, love, and I believe, fear; fear for our family. How could we survive? Our son, David 'Jeremy' Remboski, Jr., lost his battle with cancer the day before. He would have turned six that following week.

The truth was, I didn't know how we were going to survive, either. Jeremy left behind his sister Lauren, age four, and brother, Patrick, age two. There would be two other brothers who were not yet born. Thinking back, I'm sure I must have been in shock. I cried so many tears I had none left to shed. My first born was no longer with us. Unusual thoughts ran through my mind; my kids are young, I don't ever need to leave the house again or look at anyone else. I could have just crawled into bed and stayed there forever, as far as I was concerned.

Jeremy was amazing. I couldn't imagine living without him. I was so self-consumed, I couldn't help but think only about how I felt about losing him, how sad I was, what I was going to do to survive.

They say, out of the mouths of babes comes incredible truth at times. Truer words may have never been spoken. My beautiful and strong-willed daughter had so much wisdom at the tender age of four. She looked up at me one day while I was still in disbelief and uttered the words that enabled me to continue to breathe, "Mommy, now what are we going to do?"

Talk about the feeling of cold water in your face. It was then I realized it was not about me, it was about all of us-my children, his dad, grandparents, aunts, uncles, cousins and very special friends. I would need a whole chapter in this book to describe the amazing people who blessed our lives at that time. Our family and friends were looking to me thinking, I believe, if I could live through such a tragedy, so could they.

That first year was so hard. I remember thinking we weren't going to celebrate Christmas that year. How could we celebrate? Our baby was gone. Fortunately, I had a girlfriend Laura, who wouldn't let me do that. She made me go cut down our own Christmas tree, like we had always done. Between Lauren and Laura, they instilled in me the drive to pull myself through such a terrible ordeal.

During that year, I honestly don't remember much of what I did, but I do remember how I felt. I missed Jeremy so much. I would be out with the kids and someone would ask how many children I had. I would hesitate, then say three (Michael was born three months after Jeremy had passed). Lauren and Patrick would immediately correct me with their hands on their hips and say, "We have four. Our brother is in Heaven."

How do you explain to people you meet in the grocery store what happened? It seemed unreal. Our tragedy couldn't be real. I wanted the world to know about him. Jeremy was truly an incredible child. He was an old soul. His nearly six years on earth were special. He never once questioned why he had to be going through his treatments when his siblings did not. He never complained.

When I think back to how strong he was during his treatments, I believe that's where the strength I have now comes from. He was my first born, so I didn't have any other children to compare him to at the time. He took everything he was going through with amazing grace and courage. The wonderful doctors and nurses at Children's Hospital of Philadelphia, and later at Children's Hospital of Boston, all loved him. He did everything he had to do, from swallowing pills to understanding the need for his porta catheter. His questions were never, "Why?" they were always, "OK, Mommy, what's next?"

He would also ask me questions about going to Heaven. Not in a sad way but in sort of a matter-of-fact way. He loved his stuffed animals, calling them his babies. One time he asked me, "When I die, if I am holding one of my babies, will it go to Heaven with me?" He seemed to know somehow.

Jeremy's radiation treatments were at Boston Children's Hospital, one of the few places in the country that performed focal radiation on children. We resided at the Ronald McDonald House for almost nine weeks. The family who ran the Ronald McDonald House was incredible. We met so many families who truly had it so much worse than we did, with children in isolation receiving bone marrow transplants. They all received the same wonderful care.

Jeremy's cancer treatments were long and drawn out. He was able to lie very still during his radiation. There were children older than he was who had to be sedated daily. Life at the Ronald McDonald House was special to us. We ate our meals with the other families and gave each other strength and prayers. It truly was a communal feel. We all had something in common, we would have given our own lives not to have a sick child that may not get better.

Ordinarily, when a child is sick with a simple fever, your heart breaks when they are lethargic, but you know the fever will pass. Cancer is a different feeling. You would go to the ends of the earth reaching for a cure. When your child is going through treatment for cancer, you don't care if they turn off your lights, if they repossess your car or if they foreclose on your home. You thank God for every day you have and you pray for a cure.

We had clung to hopes of a positive outcome, with Jeremy's type of brain tumor having a 93% chance of being cured. He never gave up hope, doing whatever was asked of him. Many different treatments were tried and he took them all in stride. He began kindergarten in the fall of 1995, taking school very seriously. We would drive to Children's Hospital, about 45 minutes each way, for an injection of a trial drug before school. I cannot put into words how truly incredible he was. We had him in class before the bell rang at 9am.

Unfortunately, after a year, his brain tumor metastasized down his spine. Our Jeremy became one of the 7%.

Many people feel we have a sad ending… and we do. Jeremy lost his battle with cancer. However, I could have chosen to lay down and emotionally die or I could have decided to do something positive. Though we would have never volunteered our son to be the one who left this world too soon to help make another child's life a little easier, I believe that was part of God's plan. We became convinced we had to do something positive. He lived for a reason. In that spirit, we created our charity, The Jeremy Fund.

While in Boston at the Ronald McDonald House, we witnessed many families suffering financially because they had to take time from work or quit their job altogether so they could be there while their child was undergoing treatment. We were blessed with family and friends who stepped up to help us with our other children, allowing Jeremy to never have to be without his mom. I never left his side. I thank God for that every day.

We only had him for a short while, but Jeremy left an everlasting impression of love on us all. I had to make a choice. I could have chosen to feel sorry for myself and wallow in self-pity, I don't think anyone would have faulted me for that, but I just couldn't. I had to make something positive out of the worse tragedy any parent could face. We don't understand why things happen. We cannot control so much of what happens to us. We can only control how we respond. I chose to respond with something positive. We are blessed to have people in our lives who enable us to make the lives of others a little easier.

We can't take cancer or the hurting it causes away from anyone.

We can't make every child better. We can, however, try to take away some small worries. The Jeremy Fund is a non-profit organization run completely by volunteers, amazing volunteers. We raise money to help families with children undergoing treatment for cancer pay a bill or two. It's our prayer for each of them to spend more time with their child. The words 'child' and 'cancer' should never be spoken together. Until that becomes a reality, we want to do something good. Thank you Lauren, and the entire Jeremy Fund board, for helping make our lives and the lives of others just a little bit easier.

By the way, on August 28, 1998, our son Anthony was born, giving us five children, one of whom is in Heaven.

Nora Riley is an incredible spirit having an amazing human experience and loving every moment. Over the last four decades Nora has received many certifications in many healing modalities, creating a unique style of combining body, mind and spirit in healing. Nora is the owner of Pathways to Inner Healing, a multidimensional healing center in the Pocono Mountains of Pennsylvania.

Angels, Miracles and, Yes, Meditation

By Nora Riley

Angels, Miracles and yes, Meditation, the journey from the mind and ego into the heart and into the soul. Traveling upon the different pathways through this inner journey, hearts are opened, miracles unfold and lives becomes transformed.

I have seen so many miracles upon this journey through my lifetime, during which 40 plus years have been as a practitioner in the Holistic Healing field. One of the most awesome Pathways to Healing I have found in my practice is the use of meditation to help each one enter that 'sacred space within' to find the magic and the miracles which are always present, waiting to be tapped into. So many have found, when opening the gateway of their heart and their soul through the silence of meditation, anything and everything is possible. Self-Love becomes the powerful force to return one to the inner journey where the miracles appear and the Angels are there to assist toward those many seen and unseen pathways.

During the years of play/work, the joy and the return to self are the miracles I have witnessed so many find along their way, too countless to amass. Observing as many discover one of the greatest journeys of a lifetime becomes the journey back to *one's self* to the magnificence and the magic that exists within each and every one of us. That is the connection needed for healing to begin. The journey back to the Creator's fingerprint of love, light and healing, designed within every fiber and cell of one's being. The journey back to one's self, immersing within the silence of meditation is the power pack that brings balance and connection for the body, the mind and the soul.

So many of my clients have found, by silencing the mind and body and bringing awareness to their organs, cells, and self, it allows the reconnection with the true empowerment of their creation and inner healing. In meditation, people return to the realization they can relax to find support and comfort from a universe above that supports and surrounds them. I would love to take you on an inner journey within your heart and your soul to a space of reconnection with the magic of your own creation. Let's begin the pathway to Angels Miracles and Meditation.

Take a deep breath. That's it, now breathe out. Take another deep breath, exhale again. Give yourself total permission to be in this space at this time to begin the journey within. Now feel the silence slowly starting to surround you. Feel it from the top of your head to the bottom of your feet. Just relax and take the time to just 'be'. In this space of just being, envision a beautiful ball of golden energy forming above your head, a beautiful ball of energy being created as a gift designed from the realms above to be given to you. With every breath and every heartbeat, this beautiful golden ball of light fills even more. With your next inhale, allow this golden ball of light to flow down into the top of your head all the way to the bottom of your feet, bringing with it healing, light and love to fill every space within you.

Allow it to overflow within you. Once you feel you are relaxed and at ease, find that sacred space within you clearing your mind and letting go of all the chatter. In this sacred space, you will come to discover the entrance to your heart and to your soul, for it is within this space the believers find the Angels are always waiting to surround and deliver their many gifts of miracles. These gifts are golden, but cannot be bought or sold. There are no price tags, for it is here you will find they can only be obtained through the heart and soul.

From that beautiful space within your heart and soul, from that golden ball of light, envision a beautiful connection being created from that sacred space within you. From that sacred space, intend for that magical connection to flow upward, right out of the top of your head. Breathe and allow the connection to become magical, filled with love. Envision the connection becoming complete as you link with the Angelic Realms surrounding you. Feel the homecoming as you and this realm merge into one in this place of light, love and healing, the place where miracles are countless, where support and empowerment are always free and waiting to be gifted. Experience the calm, the peace and the serenity flowing to you from above.

Experience your connection, totally, from every cell, every fiber of your being. What are your worries? What are your concerns? What are your fears? What is it you no longer want to carry as the baggage you have created? This connection is the place to turn all your concerns over to your team above that wants to walk with you to ease your journey here upon earth.

Take another deep, cleansing breath, letting go of all that no longer serves you at the moment. Let go of all you carry that is not of love, light and healing. Let go of the trauma and drama that has happened during the journey of your lifetime. Just let go. Surrender to God and the Angels all that is no longer wanted. Give it over, for they are always just a breath and a heartbeat away to assist you. In this connection, in this realm, there is no limit to what you can give away.

Breathe and be in this space. Allow all to flow away through this connection to the miracles awaiting you from the realms above. This is not work. This is not hard, just breathe it all away.

When you feel you are lighter and freer from all you have given away, stay in that sacred space within your connection and ask to be filled with that golden ball of light, love and healing. Stay within this space of connection for a while and open to receive. This is the space where you connect with the Angels, the Miracles and the Gifts that are given along your way.

All you have to do is ask, believe, receive and be open to the miracles coming your way. The Angels want you to know they are always present and you are love and you are always, in all ways, loved. For it is in this space where miracles exist. You are love and you are always loved.

Made in the USA
Lexington, KY
17 November 2019